What the critics

★

A cross between a Dilbert comic ... show is full of poignant and wry observations of the working world.

—*Victoria Times Colonist*

VE Ag13

Hilarious and surreal . . . a scintillating explosion of imagination.

—*Hour* (Montreal)

★ ★ ★ ★ ★

It's not too often you see a full-house standing ovation, but *The Slip-Knot* certainly deserved the one it got. I've seen a lot of Fringe plays over the years and this easily rates as one of the best.

—*Vue Weekly* (Edmonton)

TJ Dawe can make you believe he is a truck driver, a drugstore clerk and a Canadian postal worker during Christmas rush, all simultaneously in 90 minutes . . . The young Canadian comic, reminiscent of a burgeoning Spalding Gray, has quicksilver timing and a knack for zooming in on the ostensibly mundane aspects of modern existence.

—*Charleston Post and Courier*

★ ★ ★ ★ ★

Dawe tries to make sense of his surroundings with an observational sensibility that Jerry Seinfeld would envy, and a knack for weaving stories together that would inspire quiet awe if one wasn't busy laughing so hard.

—*Winnipeg Free Press*

Dawe is an amazing talent and surely one of the best monologists plying the trade anywhere.

—*Edmonton Sun*

★ ★ ★ ★ 1/2

Rocking, raucous, rambling. . . . If Jerry Seinfeld and George Carlin had a baby, it'd be TJ Dawe.

—*Winnipeg Sun*

The Slip-Knot

The
Slip-Knot
a one-person show
TJ Dawe

BRINDLE
& GLASS

For more info on TJ Dawe or information on stage production rights visit www.tjdawe.com and www.pkfproductions.com

National Library of Canada Cataloguing in Publication
Dawe, T. J. (Ti-Jon David), 1974-
The slip-knot : a one-person show / TJ Dawe.

A play.
ISBN 0-9732481-1-4

I. Title.
PS8557.A84697S55 2003   C812'.6   C2003-906138-8

Cover and interior photos: Kim Clarke

Author's acknowledgements: Thanks to my parents. Leah Adams. Jason Overy. Everyone who worked or volunteered or billeted or paid for a ticket at the various fringe festivals where *The Slip-Knot* played. Kelly Finnegan of PKF Productions. Michael Rinaldi. Andrew Litzky and Llysa Holland of theater simple. Derek, too Shaun Mongeau. Chuck McEwen. Aviva Armour-Ostroff. Jeremy Hechtman. Brent Schiess at Just For Laughs. Zoe Randall. The Have Nots at Theatre 99, Charleston. David Ross, Janet Michael and everyone at Western Canada Theatre. Margaret Bartsch. Brian Richmond at the University of Victoria. Janet Munsil at Intrepid Theatre. Jenny Repond and David Friese at Calgary Solocentric. All of my various technicians. All the journalists whose reviews and previews helped fill the seats. And very special thanks to Ruth Linka and Lee Shedden at Brindle & Glass.

Brindle & Glass Publishing
www.brindleandglass.com

Brindle & Glass is committed to protecting the environment and to the responsible use of natural resources. This book is printed on 100% post-consumer recycled and ancient forest-friendly paper. For more information please visit www.oldgrowthfree.com.

1   2   3   4   5   06   05   04   03

PRINTED AND BOUND IN CANADA

Dedication: A Note on John Fahey

John Fahey was born in Takoma Park, Maryland (a suburb of Washington, DC) in 1939. In his teens he educated himself musically by canvassing door to door asking people if they had any old records they wanted to sell. He recorded his first album, *Blind Joe Death*, in 1959, thereby inventing a musical style that came to be known as American Primitive Guitar, in which a single steel-stringed acoustic guitar carries the rhythm and the melody. No singing. No other instruments. Fahey also had the courage to play slowly, to let the emotion be the most important thing in the song, rather than technique (although his technical playing was incredible). There was (and is) very little audience for this kind of music—mostly just other guitarists. Fahey persisted and released over thirty-five albums— many on his own label—before his death in 2001. He composed. He adapted traditional songs, blues songs, hymns, Christmas carols, a Hindu chant, part of an opera by Saint-Saëns, tracks from records no one knew but him. He constantly reinterpreted his own work. I got into him listening to his Christmas album *The New Possibility* which was one of the LPs that got toted out every Christmas season since I can remember. Really found myself appreciating it the Christmas I was nineteen. Maybe twenty. Found three other records of his in my dad's collection. Taped 'em. Started borrowing others I found in the music library at university. Couldn't get enough. Bought some. Loved 'em. Bought more. Haven't stopped. His music has long been an inspiration to me. It's some of the bravest artistic work I know of. Without a single word he says everything that needs to be said. He's voiced some of my greatest happiness. He's cradled me when I've been broken. *The Slip-Knot* is dedicated to him.

The Fahey tracks used in the show can be found on *Return of the Repressed—The John Fahey Anthology*, available in the folk section of any good music store. Although, just to be niggly, the version of *Sunflower River Blues* is from the album *Death Chants, Breakdowns and Military Waltzes*—the 1967 version (there are two on the album; the one on the anthology is yet another version).

Production Credits

The Slip-Knot premiered Saturday June 16th at noon, 2001
Venue 7 the CFCF 12 stage 4273 St Laurent

technician Diana Haynes
sound design by Jason Overy

at the St. Ambroise Montreal Fringe Festival under the benevolent leadership
of Jeremy Hechtman and Patrick Goddard.

Notes on Irregular Grammar and Punctuation

Not all lines begin with a capital letter. Nor do they all end with a punctua-
tion mark. Nor do they all reach the end of the page. Some words in the middle of sentences begin with capital letters for no reason any English teacher
would ever approve of. Many sentences are mere fragments. The Microsoft
Word version of this script is riddled with angry green underlinings. And
quite a few red ones. All of this is done to simulate the performance of the
show, the delivery of the lines. These transgressions are deliberate.

Technical notes

Lights: The opening of the show is done in a dim, cool blue wash. The actor
can barely be seen as he enters and then turns on the clip lights. After they're
all up a general wash comes up. You can still see the colour from each of the
gelled clip lights, but they're accentuation, not illumination. Until the last
five minutes or so.

Sound: The "Faith No More Loop" is about forty-some seconds of the piano
ending of the song "Epic" by the band Faith No More. It's just the piano part,
and it plays twice, looped to sound continuous, fading out at the end.
    "Christmas Bells in Hell" is a medley of various recordings (mostly
choral) of the Carol of the Bells, alternating with the main theme music from
The Exorcist.
    "Death of the Clayton Peacock" is a slow, haunting slide guitar piece.
"Sunflower River Blues" is fingerpicked and a bit more upbeat—though still
pretty dark. "Yes, Jesus Loves Me" is bright and energetic. These three tracks
are by John Fahey.

Set

Two tripods or mic stands with a total of three clip lights attached to them, around chest level. Each light is gelled—one's blue, another's green and the last one's red. They're turned off. When they're turned on, each will send a beam of coloured light at about head level on one of three spots, next to each other. This show tells three stories. The actor jumps from one spot to another, advancing each story bit by bit.

The Slip-Knot

(Lights: fade to black—10 count
Sound: Pre-show music fade out—10 count

Lights: fade in cool wash—5 count
Sound: "Death of the Clayton Peacock" in at level

The actor enters
turns on the clip lights
and stands in each position, adjusts the lights if necessary

Sound: Fade out "Death of the Clayton Peacock"—5 count
Lights: crossfade to general wash—5 count)

(1)

So at this point in the story I'd just moved to Toronto
I was crashing on a friend's couch
Winter was coming
I was looking for a job and a place to live

Whenever any of my friends in Vancouver heard that I was moving to
    Toronto they'd always say the same thing to me:
"do ya gotta place to stay?
do ya gotta place to stay
Because it's really hard to find a place in Toronto, ya know,
it's really hard to find a place in Toronto
Ya gotta place? Ya gotta place yet? Ya gotta place?"

And I'd always say:
"No I don't
I don't live there yet
I'll look for one when I get there
It's a big city
How hard could it be?"

Well, no one said anything about if it was hard to find a job there or not

So I ran out of toothpaste
Walked down the block to a Shoppers Drug Mart
And there's a sign in the window:
Position Available
So I go in
Talk to the Manager
We go to his office
He interviews me
And that's it
Hired
Like that
No application
No resume

(2)

Hello, Tracemail

Yes

Hello, Tracemail

Hello Margaret.

Yes, I understand that, but meat is uninsurable

No, I passed it on to Claims, they turned down your file, not me

No, I discussed it with my supervisor, and . . .

Yes . . .

Yes . . .

Yes, but . . .

Yes . . .

Y—

Y—

(*slump*)

mm-hmm

(1)

Now like any major corporate retail chain, Shoppers Drug Mart's got a
    "wage grid," the manager explains to me on my first day, they've got a
    wage grid
The wage grid makes sure every employee in every Shoppers Drug Mart in
    the country starts out making the same wage at the same time

Namely: Six Dollars and Forty-Nine Cents an Hour

Ahh, Fuck
I was making more than that when I was a teenager
Summer I turned seventeen I was making $9.00 an hour in a warehouse
That was almost ten years ago
Three years after that I was getting $12.00 an hour trucking
Three years after that I was making $15.85 at the post office
You like to think you're progressing
But now I'm in a new city, at the bottom of the ladder again,
And, of course, of course—I have no marketable trade skills
I can't lifeguard, or repair motorcycles, or design webpages, or burn candles
    in people's ears
The post office isn't hiring
And you can't truck in a new city where you don't know your way around
So it's this, and if it wasn't this, it'd be something exactly like it
So it's $6.49 an hour—a laughable, pathetic wage
But I don't say that to the manager as he's explaining it all to me
God, no
I smile and nod, as if $6.49 sounds Great!
Exactly what I was hoping for!

Oh, and it gets better
After three months I get a *Performance Review*
And if they like how I've been doing
Then they'll bump me up seventeen cents
To $6.66 an hour
The Wage of the Beast
I can't believe this guy's telling me this with a straight face

But the worst part is I'm smiling and nodding again

My job title, he tells me, is "Merchandiser."
I'm a Merchandiser
I've never heard of this
Kind of makes it sound like I've got a table full of merchandise and I try
    and get customers to come up and sample my fine merchandise
Nope
There's no table
But there is merchandise—plenty of it
And I take the merchandise
And I put it on the shelves
I stock shelves
I'm a stock boy
"Merchandiser" is a euphemism
But drugstores are no strangers to euphemisms
They're full of 'em

(3)

April Fool's Day—first day on the job trucking
I'm a trucker!
Not yet, not quite—two days of training first
Sitting in the cab with Brian—the head driver and co-owner of the
    company—Reliance Disposal

The job is picking up and delivering those big metal bins you see on
    the street
Not dumpsters, for any old garbage
These are specialty bins—I'm talking the big rectangular metal ones—
    green, sometimes yellow or rust-coloured, ours are green, and the
    shape of a giant Lego
And they just sit on the street, like a parked car
You know those things, they just sit there
I've always idly wondered how they get there
They're so big and so heavy
There's no wheels
Who puts 'em there?
Me!

They're for construction jobs. Reno jobs. Roofing jobs.

Our company specializes in roofing jobs
If someone's getting their roof redone, the roofers need somewhere to
      throw away the old shingles, the garbage shingles
I've never thought about that
That somewhere is one of our bins, placed right in the driveway, or on the
      street in front of the house

It rains a lot in Vancouver
So a lot of people get their roofs redone

So my Job, my Part of the World's Work, when you come right down
      to it, is:
Unwanted Shingle Get Ridder-Of-er
Helper
How's that for an obscure nook in the job market
It's like how three years ago I was a shipper/receiver in a warehouse that
      distributed equipment to insulation companies that specialized in
      removing the asbestos from the walls of old hospitals and schools
You just don't think of things like that when you're a kid wondering what
      you want to be when you grow up

(2)

yes . . .

yes, I understand that, Margaret

no, Margaret, I sent the file to Claims already

no, Margaret please listen.
I sent the file to Claims because it's over a hundred dollars—that's my
      limit—that's what my job is. Now your file is for $400, so I sent it to
      Claims—that's what I have to do. Now Claims reviewed it and they
      turned it down, and that's it! there's nothing I can do—they've closed
      the file. Even if I could reopen it—which I can't—all I'd be able to give
      you is a hundred dollars, and I know you don't want that, we've talked
      about that already

No, that's not what I'm saying . . .

Yes, I agr—

Yes, I'm with—

Yes, but if—

Yes, but—

Yes . . .

yes

Y—

Y—

(*slump*)

mm-hmm . . .

(3)

Now there's a claw, a big metal claw on the back of the truck, on an arm—
    a hydraulic arm
What you do is you pull up so the back of the truck is about five, six feet
    from the front of the bin
Then you work the hydraulic levers in the cab that send the arm back and
    then arcing down,
Then you back up a little more until the claw is right underneath the ring,
    the big metal ring welded onto the front of the bin
You lift the arm so that the claw catches the ring, and then tilts the bin
    onto the two back corners and then draws it forwards on the two little
    back corner wheels—turns out these things do have two little wheels, I
    just never noticed them before—and then pulls it up and onto the
    back of the truck
Nice, clean, easy and simple industrial process
In theory.
In practice I'm terrible at it
I've got no knack for machines, for tools, for Manly Work like this
And the hydraulic arm knows this about me
The truck knows it too
It's a simple truck: five gears, stick shift, normal brakes
Nothing I need a special kind of license for

But it's a tight stick, man
You've got to put it in exactly the right place to get it in gear
You've really gotta jam it in there, too
Any hesitation at all and it makes this AINN! noise like you just gave the
     wrong answer on a game show
It's embarrassing
and discouraging
and it's happening again and again and again and again

At the end of my two days training in the cab with Brian, two days of me
     not doing one thing right once, including getting lost in a neighbour-
     hood where I used to live
Right as I'm about to say to Brian "Listen, I'm not the right guy for this
     job, I know it, you know it, I'm sorry for wasting your time, I'll do
     something else for the summer, I'll pick raspberries or something"
The words are on the tip of my tongue—I don't get to say 'em because
     Brian speaks first, and Brian says

"Tomorrow, you're on your own"

And he throws me the keys

(1)

"Hey Bob, Lookin' Good!"

(2)

Hallowe'en.
Day one at Canada Post, and I am more tired than I have ever been in My
     Entire Goddam Life
The job I quit to take this one was at this all-night answering service
I didn't know answering services still existed since the invention of the
     answering machine, but they do, and one of 'em hired me and put me
     on the graveyard shift
Graveyards—couldn't handle that—working all night, sleeping all day, and
     then your body trying to correct itself on the weekend and starting it
     all again on Monday—couldn't do it.
So I quit

Got hired at the post office the very next day by a bizarre series of coincidences

Anyway my sleep schedule's fucked, and I have suddenly got to Stay Awake and Pay Attention for two daytime training sessions from a guy who flew in all the way from Ottawa just to train ME

The guy's reeling off technical terms and computer abbreviations and company propaganda I guarantee I will never remember but the gist of the job is this:

It's called Tracemail

I'm a Tracemail clerk in Canada Post's Pacific Division, based in Vancouver and covering the territory from Vancouver Island to Thunder Bay

Now if anyone in that thin sliver of Canada sends something Xpresspost or Priority Courier, then it's got a Guaranteed Delivery Date—it's guaranteed to get to where it was supposed to go by a certain day

If it's late and someone complains,

Or if it doesn't show up at all, and someone complains,

Or if it shows up but it's damaged, and someone complains,

Then someone from our office, the Tracemail Office, looks into it.

They check it out on the computer for the barcode scanning

They phone the post office nearest to where it was supposed to go

They talk to the supervisor

Talk to the carrier

Talk to the delivery driver

Talk to sortation

They phone the person it was supposed to go to—or, as I'm now supposed to refer to that person—the "Addressee"

They phone the RPO nearest to the Addressee

RPO?

Retail Postal Outlet—RPO—a 7-11 or a Shoppers Drug Mart with one of those little mini post offices tucked in the back corner

If the thing really was late, I can send a refund cheque for the postage they paid

If it really went missing, or showed up damaged, I can send a refund cheque for the value of the item itself, up to a hundred dollars, unless it was one of the four things Canada Post has deemed uninsurable:

Cash

Jewellery

Fragile items

and Meat.

Meat? who's gonna mail meat?

The guy talks to me for two days

I smile, nod, stay awake—barely—take a few notes and then I'm shown to
    a desk—my desk—sort of, but not quite
It's one of those four-piece desks divided by carpet partitions that you can
    tack things up on
Frequently called phone numbers
Pictures of your kids and pets
A favourite Dilbert strip someone faxed you
"Footprints in the Sand"
I've got an adjustable swivel chair
I've got a computer—a top-of-the-line 1983 computer. Black screen, green
    characters, blinking cursor—it's right out of *Wargames*
I've got a phone with a headset
I've got unlimited long-distance calling
In fact, if addressees want to check their files they can call me collect, I
    never refuse the charges
I'm supposed to tell them this, it's in my notes

I'm also the only guy in the entire office
Why this is women's work, I have no idea.
Why are bank tellers always women, for that matter? Nineteen times out
    of twenty.
Or cashiers at supermarkets and drugstores
Or running the men's underwear department at Sears
Why are restaurant kitchens full of guys?
I was a dishwasher at a high-end burger joint one summer and the kitchen
    was nothing but guys
How did this happen?

(1)

Family Planning

(3)

So that night I go to an empty parking lot with my truck and my bin and I
    practice
I practice loading and unloading
See if I can unload the bin between the white lines of an empty parking
    stall without touching 'em

And I do it
So I pick it up

And it comes on just fine

Next I take it to a lamppost
See if I can unload it and back it up within two or three feet of the lamp-
    post without touching it

And I do it again

Ladies and gentlemen, there is Hope!

Next day though, I'm flying solo

(2)

And I was right—those two days training don't mean nothin'
That guy may as well have stayed in Ottawa for all I remember and all the
    sense my notes make
But I've got twenty-five new traces,
And I'm staring at 'em with a blank face

(1)

I mean, where the hell's the Neutrogena supposed to go?
I don't see any Neutrogena at all
I never knew there were so many skin creams in my life—
Neutrogena, Oil of Olay, L'Oréal, Pond's, Nivea, Bioré . . .
I've never even heard of Bioré . . .
or . . .

(3)

Maple Ridge . . .
Well, I've driven through Maple Ridge once or twice—but I don't
    remember it
don't know my way around . . .

(1)

and then people start coming up to me and asking me where things are

Hair nets
uh . . .
Hot water bottles
uh . . .
Vicks Vap-O-Rub
uh . . .
Iodine
Iodine—I think is right over . . .

(3)

I'll just check the map book on that one
This dog-eared map book of the city of Vancouver is my best friend in
    the world
I mean, I'm delivering these bins to suburban houses
I've never heard of these streets—they're cul-de-sacs, they last one block
But how do you look in a map book while you're driving—while you're
    driving a big, ornery stick-shift truck through heavy traffic?
You wait for the red lights
But only if you actually want a light to be red
do you hit green after green after green after green

(2)

after ring after ring after ring
Ten minutes it's been ringing at this post office
It is ten minutes, I know—because there's a timer on the phone that clicks
    on every time you make a call or take a call
and in Winnipeg central post office, Station A, apparently, they think it's
    just fine to let the phone go right on ringing for Ten Goddam Minutes

(1)

right next to the band-aids, I think . . .

hold on . . .

(3)

Now, growing up on Top-40 radio, I'd hear helicopter traffic reports of
    stalls and collisions on these suburban highways I'm now driving at full
    speed for the first time in my life
I mean the burbs sprawl on and on and on
Growing up I never had any reason to explore those parts of town
They were these mythical lands to the east
It may as well have been Zimbabwe for all I knew of 'em

(1)

Hey, Paula—do you know where we keep the iodine?

(2)

Fine, don't answer. Don't answer, motherfucker. I don't wanna talk to
    you anyway
I will call . . .
the RPO nearest to the addressee—perfect
So I get out my big green binder listing all the RPOs in the country by
    order of postal code
And I call the one that looks like it's nearest to the addressee
it's Not in Service
So I call the next closest one to the addressee
and a woman answers, saying there's no post office there, and there never
    has been
So I call the third closest one to the addressee
A little kid answers

(1)

Oh—right next to the bandaids
Exactly where I was looking

thank you Paula

(3)

Now, in this map book there's two . . . *three*
There are three parallel streets in Maple Ridge
That are all called "Dewdney Trunk Road"
And they never connect up
Who drew this Map?
Satan??

(1)

Old guy hobbles up to me in aisle two
"Do you have crackera bolin?"
pardon me?
"Do you have . . . crackera . . . bolin?"

(2)

Okay—Phone the Addressee and Confirm that the Missing Item Really
    Didn't Arrive

Hello—This is Canada Post Tracemail calling about your missing item
I just wanted to make sure that it really didn't arrive
It didn't
Okay
Thank you
Good-bye

(3)

Found it! Street and address
Roofers waiting on the lawn for me—beautiful!
A complete fluke of navigation, I fully admit,
But it's my first day on the job, I'll take what I can get

So I back into the driveway, and unload my very first ever Job Site Bin . . .

all cockeyed and too far out from the overhang of the roof

(1)

Old woman comes up to me in Aisle Three, holding an identical package
   of Aspirin in each hand
100 caplets, regular strength
"Excuse me, young man—could you please tell me which one of these is
   better?"

(2)

Put the trace on hold and try the next one
Don't mind if I do
New File—
Item Arrived Damaged, Sender Wants Refund
Contents: One Ceramic Vase
or is it One Ceramic V*ahhz*—never quite sure how you're supposed to
   pronounce that word
Doesn't matter in this case, though—it's fragile
It's one of the Four Things
and that means it's uninsurable
and that means no refund
and I get to be the lucky one to call this woman and tell her

(1)

"Excuse me, but my daughter's got a rash on her foot and she's developing
   a fever—could you tell me what you would recommend for that?"

(3)

Okay, next: gotta pick up a full bin from a job site—a house on
   Warrington Crescent
Warrington Crescent . . .
So I'm driving around looking for Warrington Crescent
Can't find it
Keep going past all these teaser street signs:
Wellington Crescent . . .
Wilmington Crescent . . .
Washington Crescent . . .

Either that or street signs with branches hanging in front of 'em

(2)

Answering machine! Thank God

(1)

"Excuse me, but the only brand of cocoa butter you seem to stock here is
     your own Shoppers Drug Mart brand of cocoa butter"

(2)

Hi, this is Canada Post Tracemail calling about your damaged ceramic vase
I'm sorry to have to tell you this, but the policy with fragile items is that
"Insurance on fragile items covers loss, but not damage,"
So even though it says in the file that you purchased $100 worth of
     insurance, I'm afraid it doesn't . . . actually . . . count
"What? What? Hello? Hello? What do you mean my insurance doesn't count?"
Oh shit, she was there the whole time, she was screening her calls

(1)

"Well I don't want this brand of cocoa butter
It's not even real cocoa butter
I want the one that's made with real butter!"

(2)

"Your representative personally sold me one hundred dollars worth of
     insurance and now you're telling me it's not worth anything?!"

(3)

Brian, I can't find Warrington Crescent
I don't even know where I am

I'm lost

(1)

"The prices here are much too high
Your selection is terrible
You never stock any of the things I want
You don't even have good cocoa butter!"

(3)

"Whaddaya mean you can't find it?
Warrington's right off Dewdney Trunk Road
Just look in the goddam map book, will ya?"

(2)

"I can't believe this—you break my ceramic vase and then you have the
    gall to tell me it's my fault, My fault for sending it with you in the
    first place??
Good-Bye!!"

And slams the phone down

(3)

and hangs up

(1)

and storms out

WELCOME TO YOUR NEW JOB!!

⌒

(1)

So it turns out all of those people were right
Finding a place to live in Toronto is really hard
Finding a place while working full-time is impossible

You get up first thing in the morning
You get the paper
You scan the classifieds
You circle the ads
You call the landlords
You make an appointment to see the place after work
You go to work
You get out of work
You get on the subway
You get on the bus
You get there and it's GONE!
Taken
Rented
Too Late
Too Bad
Fucker

Unless it's a dive
And there's plenty of those in Toronto
Roaches
Mice
Rats
All of the above
Holes in the walls
Holes in the ceilings
And a giant questionable stain on the carpet the size and shape of a
    human body

And there's this one place that's hot
Really hot
I mean, it's November
Turns out it's right upstairs from the kitchen of one of those cheap slice
    pizza joints
The landlord can see I'm not too enthusiastic so he actually says
"You know, I can go downstairs and ask them to turn the pizza ovens down
    a bit"

(2)

Around this time a friend asks if I can sell his van for him
It's a maroon '88 Dodge Voyager
He calls it "Queenie"
It's got a few cracks in the windshield,
Belches out a bit of blue smoke when you first start 'er up in the morning,
Like a lot of us do
But apart from that it runs great, he tells me
Never had a single problem with her
He bought it in Calgary
Drove it to Thunder Bay and back
Now he's in Vancouver with a plane ticket for Australia
He's gotta go
Be nice to get some money for that van though, he says, you'd be doing me
      a big favour
Furthermore, there's a month left on the insurance
You've got a month to sell her and you can drive her around like she's yours
      until you do

Ah, what the hell
Vancouver's a big city
There's gotta be a lot of people out there looking for a good used van at a
      very reasonable 1500 bucks

Sure, I tell him, why not

And he throws me the keys

(1)

"Family Planning"
Family Planning is a euphemism, it's one of the euphemisms at the drug-
      store
Family Planning is a euphemism for CONDOMS
There are some other things in the section
Pregnancy tests, ovulation kits
I suppose as a section it really is Family Planning
But it's like ninety per cent condoms
The focus is on a pretty specific family plan

Ever go to a drugstore and buy nothing but condoms?
That's a lot of fun
Most people don't
Most people will avoid doing that at all costs—they'll buy things they don't
    even need, to drown out the condoms, to make it look like the con-
    doms were just one of a list of things they happened to need to stock
    up on that day
But maybe you're in a rush, maybe you're absentminded, maybe you're
    short on cash
Whatever the case may be you might suddenly find yourself at the check-
    out stand with nothing in your hand but a box of condoms
And the cashier's poker-faced
She's a pro, she knows exactly what to do
She takes 'em, blips 'em, puts 'em in the bag
Pretends not to have even noticed what your one item was
Pretends not to have judged you
Pretends not to have checked to see if they were regular-sized or large
And if they were large, pretends not have scoped out the size of your hands
    to see if you deserve them
But she noticed
And she judged
And she scoped
And she made a comment—telepathic though it was
And you heard it
And that comment most certainly was not
"Have fun Planning your Family"

"Feminine Hygiene"—or as I like to call it "Euphemism Central"
Feminine Hygiene is a euphemism for Tampons and Maxi-Pads
oh but we can't say that
Heaven forbid you should call something by its name
Even "Maxi-Pad" is a euphemism
If you look at the word "Maxi-Pad" all it means, in and of itself, is Big Pad
Sanitary Napkin just means Clean Napkin
and Maxi-Thin means Big Small—it's an oxymoron!
But we can't even call it by the oxymorons,
We have to say "Feminine Hygiene"
It's very gentle, and inoffensive
Although it kind of implies that it's for the Feminine
as opposed to the Female
Well then, does that include effeminate men?
Does that exclude butch women?

And "Hygiene"—what is Hygiene
I looked it up
Cleanliness and Appearance
Well you may as well call the whole goddam store "Feminine Hygiene," then!
At least three-quarters of the things we sell in a drugstore are exclusively for
    the cleanliness and appearance of women
Makeup, Makeup Remover
Nail Polish, Nail Polish Remover
Leg Waxing Strips—Body Sugaring Kits
Nylons—Pantyhose—Control Tops
Maternity Bras, Nursing Pads
Fancy Shampoos, Fancy Conditioners
Fancy Hairsprays, Fancy Mousses
Hair Clips, Hair Bands, Hair Elastics, Hair Curlers, Hair Dryers, Hair
    Bleach, Hair Colouring, Hair Colouring Remover
Skin Cream, Cold Cream, Anti-Aging Cream
Soaps that are made out of fruits and smell like fruits and are shaped . . .
    like fruits!
Body Mist, Body Spray,
Shower Gel, Shower Meshes
Perfume, Scented Creams, Scented Lotions
Antiperspirants and Deodorants that are "pH-Balanced for a Woman" and
    come in a slightly smaller, daintier and more feminine-coloured-and-
    shaped container than the ones for men and have flavours that always
    manage to incorporate the word "Fresh":
Active Fresh
Morning Fresh
Shower Fresh
Sporty Fresh
Baby Fresh
Powder Fresh
Ocean Fresh
Citrus Fresh
and . . .
Fresh

Not to mention tampons, maxi-pads, douches
Intimate moisturizers
Personal lubricants
as opposed to what—Impersonal Lubricants?
Public Lubricants?
And last but not least, the feminine euphemism that's only on prescription:
The Pill

At least three-quarters of the customers are women
At least
And none of these feminine products are cheap
And there's no male equivalent to most of them
I never realized how expensive it is to be a woman

Might I add, it's very few men coming in to buy the diapers and baby
    powder and baby cream, either
In this enlightened day and age
It's still always a woman by herself pushing a stroller

(3)

I'm in love
First big relationship—ohh, it's the real thing, too
You know how when you just know?
She is The One
And my first one, too
Lucky, I guess . . .

She's in Victoria—we both go to university there—that's how we met
She's from there
For all the good things about the city of Victoria, it's a really hard city to
    find a summer job in
It's full of students

So I moved back to Vancouver—just for the summer
I got this trucking job—just for the summer

We miss each other
Talk on the phone a lot

(2)

I mean, talking on the phone's what the whole job's about
And the desks are all smooshed so close together that you can hear every-
    thing anyone says
Much less anything they say over and over again
Marie-Claire, for instance, bursts out laughing at least once every five minutes
Kay tacks on a descending sigh to the end of a long laugh

Debra hangs up the phone and says "what a psycho"
Kathy with a K refers to someone being a "Happy Camper" approximately
    every fifteen seconds
Cathy with a C—her big phrase is "Been There, Done That"
Kelli with an I says "Ya" just like in the movie *Fargo*: "Ya . . . Ya . . . Ya . . .
    Oh, Ya"
Susan can't pronounce successive consonants, so "Realty" comes out
    "Reel-i-ty" and "New Westminster" turns into "New West Min-i-ster"
Sharon says "shiksh" instead of "six," and "Canada Poesht"
and her direct deshk phone number—which she is constantly giving out to
    her addressheesh is area code shiksh oh four—shiksh shiksh two, one
    shiksh eight sheven
It's a good thing for her that her name is Sharon
and not Sissy
And Donna, instead of saying "Mississaugua" says "Mississaug*wa*"

(1)

"You're Listening to the Shoppers Drug Mart Radio Network"

They've got their own radio station
Broadcast by satellite to every the Shoppers Drug Mart in the country
So that we're all listening to the same music at the same time
namely:
SMARM FROM THE EIGHTIES
Friends and Lovers
Next Time I Fall
Can't We Try Just a Little Bit Harder
Somewhere Out There
I Don't Know Much, But I Know I Love You
That's What Friends Are For
I Wanna Know What Love Is
Say You, Say Me
The Girl is Mine
Every Time You Go Away You Take a Piece of Me With You
Dan Hill
Peter Cetera
Phil Collins
Tiffany
Rick Astley
Debbie Gibson
George Michael

Lionel Richie
The Eighties
The decade taste forgot
A blight on the history of rock n' roll
Rock n Roll, man—Fuckin' Rock N' Roll! It's supposed to mean something!
Robert Johnson, Muddy Waters, BB King, Chuck Berry, Little Richard,
    Elvis, Bob Dylan, the Beatles, the Who, the Stones, Jimi Hendrix, Jim
    Morrison, Van Morrison . . .
Spandau Ballet
Amy Grant
Wham
It's the music Satan listens to while he's taking a dump

In between songs there are announcements
Not about the songs—no one cares about them—but about the store!
    What a wonderful store it is

"Welcome to Shoppers Drug Mart, We Specialize in Customer Service"
as opposed to what? as opposed to all those other drugstores where you
    walk in the door and they kick you in the teeth? As opposed to those
    stores that don't serve customers?
Any store that serves customers—and that would be . . . every single store
    on the planet—specializes in Customer Service. That term means
    NOTHING

Just like our slogan: "Price, Service, Selection—Shoppers Drug Mart"
That's it? Just "Price, Service, Selection"?
Not "Low Prices, Good Service and Wide Selection"?
we don't promise that . . .
just "Price, Service, Selection"—Three things that, for better or for worse,
    every store everywhere has—that's what makes it a store and not some-
    one's house
If you're gonna make your slogan that nebulous and descriptive, why stop
    there? Why not make it "Price, Service, Selection, Employees, Cash
    Registers, Shelves, Fluorescent Lighting, Walls and a Ceiling. Shoppers
    Drug Mart!"

"At Shoppers Drug Mart, we're concerned about your health"
BALLS
They're concerned about the money in your wallet—and that's it
If you'd like to test my little theory just go into any Shoppers Drug Mart,
    anywhere, at any time and try getting something that's important for

your health with no money in your wallet and you'll soon see what it is
that they're really concerned about.

And then my favourite announcement of all—
"Welcome to Shoppers Drug Mart—we're glad you're here"
No you're not
You don't know anything about me
I could be a shoplifter, or an arsonist, or a price checker from Pharmasave
Furthermore—you are a recording! You don't feel anything about anyone.
    So please don't insult my intelligence by pretending you do
How stupid do they think their customers are? Do they think even one
    person, in the history of Shoppers Drug Mart has stopped while shop-
    ping and said
"Did you hear that? The machine is glad I'm here . . ."
It's like when you're on an airplane and you land and you're taxiing in to
    the airport and the stewardess comes on the PA and makes the
    announcement—"Welcome to Vancouver. If this is your home then
    welcome home, but if you're just visiting then welcome to here . . . or
    wherever your final destination may be!"
Thanks
Thanks for that heartfelt form letter. Really gives me a warm fuzzy
That'd be like walking up to a stranger on the sidewalk and saying "Oh—
    pardon me—excuse me, whoever you are—but if something good
    happened to you recently, then congratulations. But if someone
    near and dear to you just died, or if you're terminally ill, then I offer
    my sympathies"
Words cease to have any meaning if you misuse them and overuse them,
    you Advertising Copy-Writing Language Pimps!

And the ads—of course there's ads—it's the Shoppers Drug Mart Radio
    Network, so guess who our one sponsor is
Ad after ad after ad after ad for Shoppers Drug Mart
And there's this one they play again and again
Never on TV, never on the radio, only on the Shoppers Radio Network
It's this guy in his backyard being catcalled by his neighbour over the fence
"Hey Bob—Lookin' Good!"
"Thanks"
"Alright Bob!"
"Thank you"
"Hey Bob, don't you get tired of all the attention?"
"Well, ever since I got my new Shoppers Optimum Card, I've been forced
    to accept that I'm a Beautiful Man"

"Oh"

"You see, I've been collecting points on my card and redeeming them for
     free stuff, like shampoo . . ."

"And that fetching cologne? (sniff, sniff)"

"Hey. Getcherself a Shoppers Optimum Card, pal . . . and get away from me"

(3)

There's a radio in the cab—and it's pretty good

Speakers are halfway decent, too

HQ wants me to listen to the Top-40 station because they have the heli-
     copter traffic reports

but I can't

It's Top-40 . . .

Instead I find this All-Jazz station out of Tacoma

Oh, it's gorgeous

Granted they play Seattle traffic reports

So I blunder into the occasional Vancouver traffic jam,

But I don't mind

It's more than worth it

I got *jazz* playing

Sounds like that get in my head and they dance around like racquetballs

(2)

There's no radio in the office—Thank God—or on anyone's desk nearby

Because you know what it would be playing:

soft rock

Music to Slip You into a Coma

The shit people play when they put you on hold is bad enough

Much less listening to "Ya," "Happy Camper" and "Mississaugwa" all day

Sounds like that they get in my head and they bounce around like ping-
     pong balls

(1)

They play this same asinine "Hey Bob" ad every hour on the hour, and
     sometimes in-between

And none of the other merchandisers hear it anymore, nor the cashiers—
    I've asked them all
They haven't heard it for months
They've tuned it out
Lucky bastards
I wish I could
But I can't
Some masochistic impulse, I hear it every single time
Sounds like that, they get in my head and they bounce around like basketballs

I've got an aural memory
If I hear something again and again—or sometimes even just once—I
    remember it
I don't know if I've always had this blessing/curse
But I do remember the first time I really noticed it
It was seven years ago
It was a very significant day in my life
Because it was the last time I ever dropped acid

(2)

I did acid for the last time four years ago

(3)

Last year I did the this really strong hit of acid and I'm never doing that again

It was powerful stuff
It was a double hit, by myself
In the daytime
Spent the day trail riding in Central Park, Burnaby
When I was peaking I was in heaven
But when I came down, as one inevitably must, I came down hard
So I lay in the grass in a field that was not too far from a road
And a car stopped at a red light
And the window was unrolled and the car stereo was playing the piano
    ending of the song "Epic" by the band Faith No More

(Sound: "Faith No More Loop" in at level)

I don't know if you're familiar with that song—it's a pretty rocking, but
    it's got this piano ending that's totally out of character with the rest
    of the song
It's haunting
And it's moody
And it left the speakers
Travelled through the air
Into my ear
And into my brain
Where it proceeded to loop

for *five hours*

(Sound: boost level, then back)

FIVE HOURS, MAN!
I thought I was going insane
I thought it was never going to stop and I was going to wind up in a
    padded cell

(Sound: boost level, then back)

I didn't
I went home
Locked myself in my room
Somehow I fell asleep
When I woke up it was gone

(Sound track should be finished by now. If it isn't, gently fade it out—10 count)

But at that point I swore that I would never ever ever ever ever ever ever

(2)

Wouldn't do acid again, uh-uh.
No Way.

(1)

Well, maybe

No.
Nah.
Probably not.

(a short pause)

(2)

Canada Post lost someone's ashes
Someone actually mailed the cremated remains of their dearly departed in a
    pre-paid Xpresspost envelope
And it never arrived

Kathy with a K's phoning all over the country looking for it
For once she is not a Happy Camper

She's really hoping she finds it too, because she doesn't have the guts to tell
    the customer that if she can't find it, they're not entitled to a refund
Because technically ashes are considered Meat
Albeit somewhat overdone

Most of our files are just on the computer, but this one's a printout
The printout's got a big yellow stripe on it
In the big yellow stripe there's one word, in block letters:
"Urgent!!!"

(1)

We're low on soap
So I load up the cart with boxes of soap from the back
Bar soap, liquid hand soap, everything
Wheel it out to aisle four, slice open the top box, draw back the cardboard
    flaps—soap everywhere
One of the bottles of liquid hand soap must've had a loose cap. Tipped and
    spilled when we were unloading it from the truck, now there's soap all
    over the other bottles
I've gotta clean 'em off
Which raises an interesting question:
What does a person use to wash away unwanted soap?
More soap?

A different brand of soap?
Dirt?

It's like Semi-Permanent hair colouring
How can something be Semi-Permanent?
It'll last half of forever??
Every other day into infinity?

or Post Raisin Bran.
That's the brand name: Post. Product name: Raisin Bran
I have no problem with that
But if you say it all together, or write it all together—Post Raisin Bran—
    then it sounds like it refers to something that happens after the
    Raisin Bran

Then this guy walks in, this big burly gorilla of a guy in a jean jacket with
    a fresh black eye, a real shiner, can't miss it, in fact, you can't look at
    anything else
The guy comes right up to me and says
"Excuse me—could you please tell me where the PMS pills are?"

(3)

The streets, roads and highways of the city of Vancouver
must've either been designed and laid out by a well-intentioned idiot
or a malicious laughing demon

The Lions Gate Bridge has three lanes
THREE?? A three-lane bridge??
and the middle one switches
arbitrarily!
the freeways have two lanes
TWO?
A TWO-LANE FREEWAY???
That's like going to a restaurant and ordering the kosher pork chop
Merging lanes that last ten feet
My goddam truck's bigger than that!
Five blocks in the suburb of Coquitlam right by Coquitlam Centre mall
    where all five intersections have lights and all five lights have left turn
    signals and left turn lanes and some of them are double left turn
    lanes—which means one direction out of four gets its own chance to go

forward or turn left while the other three directions sit there and watch
Your direction is always last
If you see your light go from green to yellow to red you're going to be sit-
    ting there watching that for a very long time
And all five of those lights are perfectly synchronized to turn red as soon as
    I fucking get to 'em!!
Road construction everywhere
Nothing ever getting any better in the slightest

And then, factor in on top of all of that the fact that you'll be very hard
    pressed to find a more evil group of human beings than any average
    random sampling of suburban commuters with their mantra
the Suburban Commuter's Mantra:
"Not in front-a ME you don't"

(1)

Shampoos and Conditioners are right next to hairspray and the hair gel,
And right across from the hair-clips and hair bands and hair elastics and
    hair dryers
It's all in one place
You can reach it from your basket
It's good marketing

Just like how the pantyhose are right next to the leg waxing strips—in case
    you change your mind

The cosmetics counter is in between the makeup and perfume in one
    direction
Between skin care and hair colouring in the other

There's more strategy to the layout of this place than I ever thought about
    when I was just a customer
Cold medicines and vitamins are at the back, near the dispensary
Family Planning's across from Baby Supplies
Family Planning's next to Feminine Hygiene
And Feminine Hygiene is next to the Chocolate

(2)

Everyone's got a nightmare file

For Kathy with a K it's the missing ashes
Susan's looking for a missing painting by Ted Harrison—an original
My nightmare is Margaret.
Margaret mailed meat. Who would mail meat?
$400 worth of venison, sent from Lethbridge to Calgary
It's two hours away—why would you mail so much meat so little distance??
Well, she proceeds to tell me—many times, over the course of many phone
    calls—she would've driven it but her car had just been repossessed
So she mailed it. Xpresspost. It was guaranteed to get there the next day
It didn't
It was delayed—as often happens with oversize, overweight packages
sat in a sortation station in Calgary—not only overnight, not only over a
    weekend, but over a long weekend
When it was finally delivered it was rotten, grey and crawling with worms
And—it was insured!
You can't insure meat—it's one of the Four Things
But a clerk at a goddam RPO, at a 7-11 postal outlet sold her $400 worth
    of insurance on the thing
Either they didn't know or they misinformed her, doesn't matter, they did,
    she paid for it, she has the receipt

So what you end up with is a retired woman—did I mention that part?
Not in the best financial straits
Who feels she's been ripped off by the post office
And has a lot of free time on her hands

I don't know any of this when I first punch up the file
It's just a regular file, it's not Urgent—they don't give me Urgents—I'm too
    new
it's just a normal file—there's a bare-bones description in the summary
So I call her up
And she proceeds to tell me her sad tale of woe
But it's only about three or four minutes long, and she's looping it
over and over again
seemingly inadvertently
for thirty-six minutes and counting
and she's not running out of steam

I finally find a tactful way to end the conversation

Whoo

Pause

Phone rings

Hello, Tracemail?

It's her!
She called me right back!
She Star-69-ed me

(1)

Still haven't found a place
What's the matter with this city?

I've been on the one friend's couch for two weeks now—it's a bit much to ask

So I move in with Marty and Tina, my only other Toronto friends
They're a married couple
They're super nice
And the best part is—they have a guest room

(2)

Having the van ends up being kind of fun
I've had my license since I was sixteen, I've had four different driving jobs,
    but I've never owned a car before
Now I do
Now if it's sunny I bike to and from work
But if it's raining, which it is more often than not—in Vancouver, in
    November—I drive

No one wants to buy it though
I'd think about buying it myself if I could afford it
One guy walks by, looks at it, offers me 800 bucks cash, right then and there
Eight hundred—from fifteen?
I can't go that low, it's not even mine
How about twelve?
Nope—not willing to bargain at all
Walks away

Okay
But after him—no walk-bys, no calls, nothing

So I buy bigger "For Sale" signs
Put 'em in all the windows
I take out ads in all the papers
Even put my Canada Post work number on 'em

(3)

Phone calls with my girlfriend start getting kind of stiff
There's nothing to say
A year ago, we'd be talking on the phone three or four hours a day
And we lived in the same city that summer—we'd have seen each other the
    same day
Now it's hard find things to talk about
Am I gonna tell her about what bins I delivered?
Am I gonna turn into one of those guys that comes home and can only
    talk about what happened at work that day?
I don't care about this job
It's nothing to me—it's a paycheque—that's all
It's a sausage grinder eating up my summer

But after a while you notice that this joooooooob has annexed a portion of
    your brain
That this waste of time comes with terms, and forms and procedures that
    you just have to know
And these terms and forms and procedures have taken up parking spots
    inside your head
Big bins
Medium bins
Little bins
and the short wide squat bins for asphalt, gravel, chunks of cement and
    deliveries of rocks

(2)

Regular traces
Urgent traces
Signature retrievals on registered letters

File summaries
Claims reports

(1)

Fragrance free
Original scent
Softly scented
With aloe vera
With vitamin E
With a bonus 20%, Free!

(3)

You wake up and you find yourself thinking about these things

(2)

Refund by postal products
Refund by cheque
Letters of explanation
Letters of apology

(3)

Tarps
Bungee cords
Safety chains
Metal doors
Locking handles

(1)

For dry skin
For sensitive skin
For damaged skin

With special moisturizing ingredients
With special therapeutic ingredients
With special medicinal ingredients listed in a really small font that you
    can't read and don't know what they mean anyway
With a bonus 33%, Free!

(3)

It's not really that hard of a job
Pretty much anyone could learn how to do it
Just like how pretty much anyone could learn how to drive, or type, or
    read, or make lasagna if someone worked with them for a bit and
    showed them how

(2)

Solved traces
Deleted traces
New traces
Urgent traces
Traces sent to Claims

(1)

For normal hair
For oily hair
For dry hair
For coloured hair
For permed hair
For damaged hair
For frizzy hair
For split ends

(2)

It's just a certain amount of specific information that you have to memorize
    and then be able to belch back on command
Just a new system to find your way around in

(3)

Fast lanes
Slow lanes
Merging lanes
HOV lanes
Paved shoulders
On-ramps
Off-ramps
Overpasses
Underpasses
Yield signs
Stop signs
Slow signs, held on a stick, by a woman in a reflective orange vest and a
    hard hat

(2)

You realize there's no special reason why you've got this job over anyone else

(1)

Fresh scent
Fresh surf
Musk
Original
Unscented
Avalanche
Wild rain
Sea breeze
In a roll-on
In a clear gel
Invisible
Goes on dry
Long-lasting
Non-marking
pH-balanced
With a bonus 66%, Free!

(3)

So you set aside a bit of your brain and you learn this series of details
And pretty soon you can do it—
You can navigate this new grid without even having to think about it

(2)

In-office calls
Inter-office calls
Local calls (dial 9)
Long-distance calls
Collect calls
Voicemail codes
Computer codes
Start-up codes
System codes
Security codes for the office door, the bathroom door and the elevator

(1)

Non-drowsy
Night-time
For dry coughs
For congestion
For sneezing, itching, fever, coughing, stuffed-up sinuses and a runny nose
With a bonus 70% free!

(2)

And then one day you wake up and you find you've got these things tat-
    tooed on the inside of your eyelids

(1)

For allergies
For bad backs
For sore muscles

For arthritis
For osteoporosis
For yeast infections
For hemorrhoids
For warts
For diarrhea
For constipation
For upset stomach
For gas
For the immune system
For nursing mothers
For nursing infants
For improved memory
For weight loss
For muscle gain
For overall health
For total nutrition
For gaps in one's dietary intake

(2)

You go somewhere for lunch
But you can't leave it behind

(1)

For aches & pains
For strained muscles
For sprained muscles
For surface infections
For rashes & insect bites
For eczema
For athlete's foot
For corns, calluses and bunions
For grey hair
For loss of hair
For removing hair
For dandruff
For fungal infections
For ingrown hairs
For ingrown toenails

For insomnia
For chronic fatigue
For lack of energy
For acne
For depression, moodiness and PMS
With a bonus 75%, Free!

(2)

You take it with you on the weekend

(3)

Discarded shingles
Shingle wrappers
And the wooden pallet the shingles come on
Roofing nails
Cigarette butts
Subway wrappers
McDonald's wrappers
Plastic wrappers for pepperoni sticks
Pop cans
Beer cans
Coffee cups
Slurpee cups
And the vague scent of roofers' piss

(2)

It creeps up on you on a day off

(1)

Alcohol-free
Sucrose-free
Lactose-free
Pill-shaped
Capsule-shaped
Gel-caps

Easy-to-swallow
Easy-to-chew
Orange-flavoured
Grape-flavoured
Wild berry burst
With a childproof cap

(3)

And then you notice a bin from another company in someone's driveway
But it's crooked
And it's too far out from the overhang of the roof

(1)

With alpha hydroxy
With aloe & lanolin
With balsam & protein
With wheatgrass
With raspberry
With chamomile
With watermelon
With juniper berries and a picture of a cute cartoon bug sitting on a leaf

(2)

And then you get a letter from a friend
And you notice that the postal code's written on the wrong line of the
    envelope

(1)

With primrose & thyme
With lavender & mint
With red clover & wild ginger
With citrus & rosemary
With witch hazel & honeysuckle
With cherry bark & Irish moss

With tea tree oil & sage
With hops, apricot & almond
With sunflower, honey & hibiscus
With vitamin E, carrot & milk protein
With the extract from wild strawberries
With the extract from the queen bee
With extract from the rectum of the rhesus monkey
With a bonus 100 ml bottle, Free!

And then you go into a different drugstore
But the shelves aren't faced
And the toothpaste is understocked

Regular
Super
Super-plus
With extra absorbency
With added absorbency
With super absorbency
With wings
With added thickness
With added softness
With double rolls
With six extra rolls, Free!

(2)

and you think—why do I care?
Why should any of this matter to me in the slightest?
How much of my brain is this taking up?

(1)

On sale
20 cents off
30 cents off
50 cents off
80 cents off if you buy two
90 cents off if you buy three
With 100 bonus points

With 200 bonus points
With 500 bonus points if you buy five
Limit of four per customer

(2)

Then it hits you that it'll never end
There's no concluding date to this project

(3)

Diesel stains
Gas receipts
Gas cards
Card-lock cards
Oil checks
Oil rags
WD-40
And a can of ether in case the engine won't start

(2)

There's no graduating and there's no moving on
There will never come a day when all the packages have been found and
    dispatched to their proper destinations

(1)

Flexible hold
Firm hold
Extra-firm hold
Non-aerosol
Aerated
Accents
Highlights
Adds lustre
Adds bounce
Adds shine

(3)

When the roofs have been redone
And the houses renovated
And all the garbage finally cleared to where it's supposed to go

(1)

With a mail-in rebate
With a coupon
With a built-in discount
With easy-to-follow instructions
With a money-back guarantee
With a 1-800 helpline
New and improved
Not tested on animals
Ozone-friendly
As seen on television
As used in hospitals
As recommended by doctors and pharmacists
As recommended by Dr. Mom

And there will never come a day when all the people everywhere are
        healthy, clean
and have all the health and beauty products they will ever need

Restores nature's balance
Eases tension
Reduces stress
Solves problems
Performs miracles
Regenerates severed limbs
Wakens the dead
Reverses time

(2)

This is a giant machine

(1)

Saves marriages
Gives back one's youthful looks and libido
Raises kids to be happy, healthy, faithful to their parents, non-alcoholic,
    drug-free and heterosexual

(2)

And I am nothing but a single cog on a single wheel
Amidst millions and millions and millions of wheels
Spinning and spinning and spinning and spinning

(1)

Deciphers the lyrics to Louie Louie
Translates Etruscan
Understands and explains *Finnegan's Wake*

(2)

I am not an integral component

(1)

Cures everything
Solves everything
Knows everything
Loves everything

(2)

I am immediately replaceable

(1)

Listens

Understands
Validates
Doesn't judge

(2)

And my life, my problems and my experiences are not unique

(1)

And provides a constant, daily reassurance
To anyone and everyone
That all trials will end in success

(2)

And the world would go on just fine if I suddenly wasn't in it or had never
    been in it at all

(1)

The Good Guys Will Win

(2)

And as I realize this

(1)

Your Dreams Will Come True

(2)

All I can do is stand there and watch
the hours and the days and the weeks

(1)

And Everything, Everywhere

(2)

And the months and the years

(1)

Will Turn Out OK,

(2)

Peel away
and slip down the drain

(1)

For Everyone

(2)

Like so many popped soap bubbles

(1)

Amen.

With a bonus 5000%, Free!

⸴

(1)

Sometimes the music just stops
Fades out
No ads, no songs from the eighties

Just five seconds of silence

And then it comes back

I ask the manager about it and he says sometimes there's a problem with
     the satellite
I don't know—maybe it passes behind anther satellite or something

Signal gets blocked for a bit

Five seconds of silence
Sometimes our dish even picks up the signal from another satellite
So you get a taste of an altogether different kind of music

And sometimes it's even something good

(Sound: Bring in "Sunflower River Blues" at level, play to the end of the track.)

And it's made all the sweeter because it's so rare
So hard-won

Like a pitcher of fresh-pressed apple juice in the desert
Like rain from heaven
Like a flower growing through a crack in the pavement

(2)

Trace comes up
Addressee's in Victoria
And I recognize the street name
It's where my ex-girlfriend lives
I even recognize the postal code
This person's on the same block

We were in love

Three years ago
A million years ago
I thought she was The One

I wonder how she's doing

(3)

HQ sends me on a delivery out to the Burrard Thermal Plant
It's this big power station out in the sticks
They always have a bin there
Every week you bring 'em a new one, take back the old one
And it's a nice long drive through the woods and along the water
And there's no cars, no houses, no people at all
Just tall evergreens
Like sentinels in the wind

(1)

Why the eighties?
If the Shoppers radio network wants syrup, they can find it in the music of
    any decade at all—why are they so faithful to that one?
Well—think of all those young moms that come in pushing their
    strollers—how old are they?
Twenties and thirties.
How old were they when this eighties music was first popular?
Kids and teenagers
Same as me
And as much as I despise eighties music, I can't deny it does bring a certain
    kind of nostalgia
Because that's when I used to listen to that music—a lot
So it'll take me right back to when I was a kid
Back when everything mattered so much
But a big problem was something like homework
Or getting a detention
Or your mom making something you didn't like for supper that night
Back when if you had a job, it was fun!
You got to spend your paycheque on whatever you wanted
All of it
Every time!

Before there was rent
Before there were bills and responsibilities
Before the weight of the world tried to crush you into gravel

When you're a kid, the music you hear, it stamps itself on you, even if it's
    something really bad
And as I'm stocking those shelves, all it'll take is a certain synthesizer lick
Or a saxophone solo
Or a meaningless, unintelligible lyric about love that I haven't heard since it
    was coming out of my black transistor radio on my desk while I doing
    my grade six fractions multiplications
And I'm right back there

Back to that time
When there was so much hope
So much energy
I never slept in
I sprang out of bed—couldn't wait to take on the day
Summer lasted forever
Grown-ups knew everything
Every direction stretched off to infinity
And every story ended with a victory

(2)

Christmas

At the post office Christmas incorporates not only all of December, but all
    of November
That's why I'm here—I'm a Christmas temp
And right from day one, on Hallowe'en, I could hear people talking about
    how the volume was really going up
I didn't notice—I was new
I was just learning to walk on my wobbly legs
And I'd see Cathy with a C bringing those yellow Urgent files to other peo-
    ple's desks, but never mine and that was fine with me

Well, things are different now
Even I'm noticing how busy it is
And even though people don't write letters anymore, they still send
    Christmas cards

And because of people ordering things off the internet, we're told that
	Canada Post is handling its highest number of packages ever this year
	by quite a bit
That means they're losing their highest number of packages ever this year,
	by quite a bit
Pretty soon Cathy with a C starts bringing some of those yellow Urgent
	files to me,
One after the other after the other after the other

And it's only the third week of November

(1)

Which you'd think might be a little early for a Christmas blitz, but we're
	doing it
Guess it makes sense in the retail world
After Hallowe'en, start hocking Christmas
In a way I'm surprised we've left it this long

But now we're doing it—we've got garlands and plastic evergreens all over
	the store
Fake snow spraypainted on the fake windowsills
"Ends"—end displays of wrapping paper and plastic Santas and Santa cards
	and Santa hats
And chocolates—this massive truckload of Christmas chocolates comes in
Manager tells me we sell almost as many chocolates at Christmas as we do
	at Easter
Which is pretty good for Jesus, I think—the Son of God, and one hell of a
	chocolate salesman

And the Shoppers Drug Mart Radio Network has switched its programming
to
Christmas carols

White Christmas
Holly Jolly Christmas
Have Yourself a Merry Little Christmas
Silent Night, by Stevie Nicks
Santa Claus is Coming to Town, by the Beach Boys
Do You Hear What I Hear, by Whitney Houston
Christmastime is Here, from the Charlie Brown Christmas TV Special—

which, if you hear it out of context and with no dialogue overtop, goddam saddest song ever recorded
The Shoppers Drug Mart Christmas Carol—written and recorded especially for the Shoppers Radio Network—without a doubt the vilest
thing I've ever heard
And then there's my favourite Christmas carol of them all: the Christmas
Carol from *The Exorcist*

(3)

Christmas for roofers, that's what they call the month of May in the industry
For some reason that's when everyone wants a new roof
HQ raises my pay—twelve bucks an hour
Hey! Most money I've ever made doing anything
Didn't even ask for a raise

But it's gonna get busy, they warn me, Really Busy
We'd like you to start parking your truck at home every day after work so
you can leave first thing in the morning whenever we give you the call

Okay
We'd also like it if you could work weekends
Just for this month
Including the long weekend

Sure . . .

(1)

You know—the Carol of the Bells
Everybody knows the Carol of the Bells . . .
The version they play on the Shoppers Radio Network is a choral
And it sounds like someone slipped that choir something—they are wild-
eyed and intense

Ring Christmas Bells, Merrily Ring
Tell All the World, Jesus Is King
Ring Christmas Bells, Merrily Ring
Tell All the World, Jesus Is King
Ya-dada-dada Ya-dada-dada Ya-dada-dada Ya-dada-dada

Have a merrymerrymerry CHRISTMAS . . .
Have a merrymerrymerry CHRISTMAS . . .
RING
RING
RING
RING . . .

Scariest Christmas Carol in the World!
And it's made even worse by the fact that I think it's really similar to the
    theme music from *The Exorcist*
Which they'd just re-released in the movie theatres—"The Version You've
    Never Seen"
Which was an accurate description for me, because I'd never seen it
So I went
Fucking terrified me!
I mean, not only is that a scary movie completely by its own merits, but by
    the standards of that movie I was a prime candidate for possession
    when I was eleven
I was a good, pious Catholic kid
I was an altar boy, I went to mass six days a week—by choice!

And in the movie—which has been corroborated by actual exorcism-
    performing priests as being very accurate—apart from the head twist-
    ing in a full circle—in the movie, when they finally get the devil out
    of the little girl, they say she doesn't remember any of it
They're very emphatic about that point—She Does Not Remember Any
    of It
Well good, thank God
No—Wait a Minute—Bad
Think of what that implies
If she didn't remember it then neither would we
Therefore that could've happened to any one of us
And if the people around us had kept it quiet—and you bet they would
We still wouldn't know!

(3)

Things with my girlfriend only get worse
Tension
Pauses
Awkward silences

Groping to keep the conversation going
She doesn't laugh at my jokes anymore,
It's like throwing darts at a brick wall
Nothing I say sparks us on to talk about anything
And I'm a talkative guy

What's happening?

Two months ago everything was fine

Long Distance Relationships Suck

(1)

I found a place!
Oh, thank God
Friend of a friend, in a house
He's got three roommates that are all moving out at the same time and
    they're buying a place together
He's not—he's staying—he wants three new roommates
I might be one of 'em
The neighbourhood's great: Parkdale
It sounds so pastoral!
And the house is great
The rent is cheap—less than I was paying in Vancouver, anyway
And the room I'd be taking is huge—hardwood floors, high ceiling, big
    window facing the street—part of it's stained glass
And a fireplace—a Fireplace in my Room!
I'll Take It!

But there's a catch, he tells me, there is a catch:

It's not available until February

(2)

End of the month coming up, still no takers on the van
The insurance is rapidly running out
Okay, I'll just re-insure it for a month in my own name and keep trying

But I can't, the insurance woman tells me
First I have to get it inspected
Inspected?
It's an out-of-province vehicle
It's registered and insured in Alberta
It has Alberta plates
Before it can be insured in BC it has to pass inspection by a licensed
     BC mechanic
Just a formality, she tells me

Alright, I'll get it inspected then

But let me warn you, she says, those cracks on the windshield? automatic
     failure

So I replace the windshield
400 bucks
That's fine . . .
I'll just deduct that from the fifteen or the twelve or the ten or whatever I
     end up selling it for

I get it inspected
100 dollar inspection fee
I'll deduct that too

Except it FAILS

It's got a busted reverse light, the brake cable's worn, and it belches out blue
     smoke whenever you start 'er up
Well, shit.
They don't mind any of that in Alberta

Well now what
Should I just sell it to a used car dealer, see what I can get—at least try and
     recoup my 500 bucks?

Yup

(1)

Okay—so now all I've gotta do is find a place for December and January

Shouldn't be too hard
But all the rooming houses and cheap hotels are full
No one's subletting for such an odd period of time—December and January
Every apartment has a year-long lease, unbreakable
And no one who wants a roommate wants a two-month roommate—
    understandably
I could lie—but I just can't screw someone over like that.
And in a big city like Toronto there's only one place for short-term
    accommodation.
One!
Furnished Bachelor Suites starting at a mere $1500 a month
What??? $1500 for One Month?
I'm a merchandiser
That's almost double what I earn
And I'd have to stop eating

(2)

And Margaret calls

Hello Margaret

mm-hmm . . .

mm-hmm . . .

mm-hmm . . .

I don't argue with her anymore
Just let her run on, she will anyway, what's the point?

She's been calling my supervisor
She's been calling Claims
The Canada Post Ombudsperson actually hung up on her
The company president is refusing to accept her collect calls (surprise, surprise)

I've gotta help her, she says
I'm the only one who listens, she says,
Who's treated her with even an ounce of decency,
Is this how Canada Post treats the elderly?

But there's nothing I can do!
My supervisor asked me about this file because I'd been working on it for
    so long
She looked at it and said
"You shouldn't have this
this is over a hundred dollars—this should have gone straight to Claims
It's a mistake that this was given to you in the first place
You're not allowed to work this file anymore"

Thank you!!!

But try telling that to Margaret

Meanwhile Cathy with a C is putting one yellow Urgent file on my desk
    after another
Missing airline tickets
Missing passports
Missing heart medication
Urgent! Urgent!

(3)

"Shit! What the fuck wuzzat!"

You know that feeling when your stomach just turns into liquid and goes
    whaaaa . . .

I'm backing up a bin into a driveway in Surrey
I can't quite see because of the hanging branches from the hedges that've
    never been trimmed
One of the roofers is waving me in
Now maybe I didn't see his signal for "stop"
Maybe he just was talking and gesturing to someone else the whole time
and BANG!
Back corner of the bin whacks the front corner of the house
This big chunk of stucco falls off
The owner of the house inside hears it and feels it
Comes running out the front door
This big tattooed bald guy in a wife-beater, yelling at me

(1)

Friday, last day of the month
Still no possibilities on a place
What am I gonna do?
I haven't got the slightest idea

Getting ready to leave for work

There's a note

In an envelope

On my shoes

Addressed to me
From

Marty

(2)

Friday
Last day of the month
On my lunch I don't even leave my desk
I'm phoning used car dealers out of the Yellow Pages
Ya wanna van? Ya wanna van? How bout you? Ya wanna van?
Miracle! One of them's interested
He's asking questions about papers, insurance papers, ownership papers

And here's where it gets ugly

Uglier

It turns out I don't actually own this van, not legally

And neither did my friend.
He's not a Canadian citizen
He bought it through a friend in Calgary—she paid for it with his money,
    signed the papers and then transferred ownership to him with a hand-
    written written statement on a sheet of paper, signed in ink

He transferred it to me with a hand-written statement on a sheet of paper,
    signed in pencil
The used car dealer and the Insurance Corporation of British Columbia
    will not accept a hand-written statement on a sheet of paper, even if it's
    signed in blood

So the Calgary friend still owns it
She's the only one who can sell it
Her name, address and phone number are on the form
Sheila Sanderson

So I call her up

And the number's Out of Service.

So I call Calgary Directory Assistance

Hello, do you have a listing for Sheila Sanderson, please?
"That number's unlisted, Sir"

Any chance you could give it to me anyway?
I'm not a stalker,
I'm trying to sell a van . . . it's . . . it's really important.

"I'm sorry, we can't do that, Sir"

(pause)

I have her address

"we don't give addresses, sir"

No, I know that—*I* have her address
If I were to read you the address that I have
Is there any way
Even just by coughing
That you could confirm
If she still lives there or not?

Please?

(3)

Friday—last day before Victoria Day long weekend—first day of Victoria
    Day long weekend, really, except it's the morning, but you get the idea

Girlfriend and I were up late last night on the phone
Fighting
I didn't sleep too well
HQ called me early
I've been on the road since quarter to six
And it's raining—hard

And coming up on this intersection
There's this dumb-ass bus
Making a left turn on a red
What the hell?

(*screams*)
My light was red. His was green
How did I not process that?
I slam on the brakes and screech to a halt right over top of the second
    white line of the crosswalk

If there'd been anyone walking

I'd've killed 'em.

(1)

I can't read the note
I can't
I've been with Marty & Tina for two weeks now
And they're totally nice, never once have they made me feel like I'm
    imposing in the slightest
But two weeks is a lot to ask—much less two months

That's what this is about, I know

Not now
Read it later
Sometimes the only chance for a moment of peace is to delay the inevitable

So I put on my shoes, my coat, my scarf and my hat
And go to work
And at work there are big green letters markered onto the staff notice board:

Don't Forget About the Staff Party Tonight!

(3)

I'm not supposed to make long-distance calls on the truck cel, much less
    personal long-distance calls, but I'll explain later, I'll pay for it all
I'm on the phone with my girlfriend all day
arguing, apologizing
arguing, apologizing
arguing, apologizing
arguing, apologizing

In the middle of all this HQ sends me out to the Burrard Thermal Plant
When I get there this guy in a hard hat and a slicker comes running up to
    the truck
"Yer gas cap's gone—yer spilling diesel all over the place"

W-what?

I get out and look
And he's right
The gas cap is not there
Now it's raining—the pavement's wet—and there's a long rainbow stripe
    that shows exactly where I've been driving on the lot
I just fueled up before I came here
I was arguing on the truck cel the whole time
Did I forget to put the gas cap back on?
Have I been splashing diesel all the way here from the card-lock station???

(2)

Got it, got it
The Operator coughed
Confirmed the address

Okay, Sheila Sanderson, I now have your street address

So, today, after work
I'll drive to Calgary

I will drive this goddam van to Calgary
I'll find this woman
And get her to sign the transfer form
It's a flimsy thread, I know
But it's my only chance

(3)

It's okay—it's okay
They found the cap about fifty feet back
Must've been on crooked and worked its way off on the long drive here
The spill isn't that big
They can clean it, they say
They have equipment, they say
The cleanup cost shouldn't be any more than eight or nine hundred dollars

I phone HQ, tell 'em what I did
Please fire me
please

And they give me my schedule for the next day

They don't need me until ten AM
Ten?
Of course—it's Saturday of a long weekend
And last delivery today is in . . . Delta
Right next to Tsawassen
Where you get the ferry to . . . Victoria
Ninety-minute crossing
Leaves every two hours
I'll ferry over tonight, patch everything up, have sex, and catch the seven
    AM ferry back tomorrow morning

(2)

Four o'clock, I'm out the door, on the road

It's a ten-hour drive from Vancouver to Calgary, I've done it before
Maybe eleven or twelve hours, if you're not lucky

Insurance runs out at midnight
Shouldn't be a problem
I'll be in the middle of nowhere
It'll be dark
No one'll be out
And quite honestly, who reads license plate tags?

(1)

A staff Christmas party
In a specially rented bar

Perfect timing
Whenever I'd have a dream that I was falling into a bottomless pit, or slip-
    ping down a slope—I always found it was a better strategy instead of
    trying to scramble back up to dive right in to the centre

So let's go to this staff party, tonight of all nights
And let's do something I haven't done in a long time
Let's get really wrecked

(2)

Five-thirty and I'm outta town
Took one of the smaller roads and it wasn't so bad
Used to be a trucker
I know a few things about the traffic patterns in the city of Vancouver
One of them is that there is nothing worse than the #1—the Trans-Canada
    Highway
Heading east on a Friday afternoon

(3)

of a goddam long weekend
It's Victoria Day long weekend, so apparently the entire city of Vancouver
    has upped, en masse, and decided to go to Victoria together!

It's five-thirty
I missed the five o'clock sailing just sitting in the line-up
Only two sailings left: the seven and the nine
Radio's saying there's a three-sailing wait
How's that work?
Maybe it's different if you're in a big truck

(1)

Five-thirty—half an hour before punching out
Pete—this other merchandiser—asks if I'm going to the party

Yup
Good, he says
Cuz I've got something special

(2)

Just past Chilliwack, it's dark already
On the radio I found the all-jazz station from Tacoma I used to listen to
        when I was trucking
And then a siren—red and blue lights
What—no!—what did I do??
It's not midnight—I'm not speeding—what?
And the cop catches up
And pulls over the guy in front of me

(3)

I finally make it to the ticket booth
All sailings are full, the woman says
Even for trucks?
Especially for trucks
Nooo . . .
Walk-on! Can I get on as a walk-on
Sure, she says, if you can find a place to park that thing
Good point
It's a long weekend—the parking lot there's been full all day—probably
        all week

And the ferry terminal's on this long skinny peninsula
And every inch of the side of the road going all the way Tsawassen is solid
    parked cars, bumper to bumper
All these people that parked and walked on, just like I wanna do
Chances are one in a thousand that I'll find a spot
One in a million I'll get one big enough for this giant fucking truck

(1)

Pete and I punch out at the same time
We're walking to the bar
Neither of us have ever been there but we've got the little photocopied map

So Pete—what's the something special
Pete pulls out his wallet
Unsnaps the change flap
Takes out a piece of crinkled aluminum foil, folded over itself
Unfolds it
Presents it
Two little pink square tabs

"Anyone for acid?"

Oh, Jesus Pete
I haven't dropped acid in years
Not since the Faith No More time
And I swore on my soul that I would never ever ever ever ever do it again
ah . . .

FUCK IT

(2)

Through the valley and into the mountains
It starts to snow—just a bit, but it's sticking
Does this van have snow tires?
Take a wild guess
Okay, okay—just take it nice and slow and easy

(3)

Driving slow as I can, up and down that peninsula looking for a spot to park
No luck, no luck at all
Couldn't even park a scooter
So into Tsawassen I go

But the city of Tsawassen has had to deal with people like me many times
    and they're ready
No Parking signs everywhere
Will Tow signs, Impound signs, Time Limit Strictly Enforced signs
And if there's any time where they really will enforce it, it's a long weekend
It's Victoria Day long weekend, first long weekend of the season
Christmas for tow trucks
Wouldn't that be just dandy if I got the company truck towed

So deeper and deeper into residential Tsawassen I go
Until I find a nice, quiet cul-de-sac
And park in front of an unfinished house

(1)

"Fuck It"—very powerful words
You could have the strongest resolve in the world, with the best reasons, the
    most solid rationalizations and tie-ins to your Guiding Life Principles
And all it takes for a grand, complete and instant veto is
Ah, FUCK IT

Acid at the Christmas party
How apropos
Chemicals to help celebrate with the fellow employees of a pharmacy

To make it even better I should take a Tylenol 3, drink some cough syrup,
    and pop a few Gravols
Gravol . . .
To make a personal confession I have done Gravol recreationally,
(that's Dramamine for any Americans out there)
I was hanging out with my acid-head friends in Burnaby
I'd never done acid
I wanted to
So did they

They couldn't get any
So we did Gravol instead
It was their idea
They'd done it the night before, they said it was a lot of fun
So we did it
Nine tabs of Gravol each, all taken at the same time
You'd think it would put you to sleep
Nope
Took three or four hours to kick in, but when it did
BOING!

Only did it one other time after that
It was three years ago
I was particularly desperate
I was driving to Calgary

(2)

What else can I do, man?
It's coming up on ten and all this snow's slowing me down so bad I'm not
     even halfway there
Nine tabs of Gravol it is
Washed down with the provocative mixture of Dr Pepper and instant
     coffee grounds
Caffeine kick comes pretty quickly
Gravol kick's gonna take a while—that's okay—I'm still pretty awake

Lemme tellya, a road trip's a drag after dark
There's no scenic beauty, not even in the mountains of BC
All you can see is the tiny little bit of road your headlights show
And the headlights coming the other direction
And the tail-lights in front of you
The red tail-lights
The distant red
The gentle, soothing red . . .
Uhh!!! (*shakes awake*)

(3)

Hi, could I have a cab to the ferry

I'm at Tsawassen Town Plaza
at the payphone in front of the Mailboxes Etc

I'm pretty easy to spot, I'm the sopping wet guy standing in the pouring
    rain like a nut

The ferry terminal

The Tsawassen Ferry Terminal

It's the one in Tsawassen!

(1)

It takes Pete and I longer to find the bar than we figured, but we eventually
    get there
We walk in the door
And it's a great party
There's food, and it's free and there's drinks, and they're free—first two, anyway
And there's people—
It's everyone from work, but in normal clothes, no uniforms, no name tags

(Sound: bring in "Xmas Bells in Hell" at level)

No chance anyone will come up and make any of us go root through the
    basement for their favourite kind of enema bag
And there's laughter
And there's smiles
And there's presents from our Secret Santas
And cards that people signed their names to
And—oh—could it be any more perfect?
It's the song
Hey Everyone!
Everyone! Shut up! It's the fucking song!
It's the Christmas Carol from *The Exorcist*!

And Urande from Cosmetics comes up and says
"There's no music playing"

(2)

Now, heading east on the Trans-Canada Highway towards Calgary, the
    worst of it are these two mountain passes
Rogers Pass and Kicking Horse Pass
Before them is Revelstoke, BC,
Between them is Golden, BC
After them you're in Alberta, Banff National Park

I stop in Revelstoke, fuel up, piss, buy peanuts and Powerade and drive off
And as the clock hits midnight
I'm climbing Rogers Pass

(3)

Half an hour and two more phone calls later the cab finally shows up
So I missed the seven
One ferry left: the nine

Hi
I would like to go
To the walk-on passengers' ticket booth
Of the ferry terminal
Please

(1)

Whoa
It's here—it's here (it's here!)
And it's been a long time coming

Do something normal
Sit down
Read
The placemats on the tables have "Fun Christmas Facts" on them
Mine says:
"The name 'Santa Claus' is an American phonetic mispronunciation of the
    German and Dutch 'St. Niklaas'
The actual historical St. Nicholas lived in Asia Minor—Turkey—in the
    4th century AD.

The modern image and costume of Santa Claus were created by the Coca-
    Cola Company"

(2)

Snow's falling with a vengeance
I'm taking it sloooooooow
And Whoosh! this green van zips by

Good luck to ya, pal

It's actually kind of inspiring to see someone drive with that much confi-
    dence over the snow
A trailblazer like that makes you think maybe the road's not so treacherous
Maybe I'll make it

(1)

So imagine—just imagine—if you could go back in time and meet the
    young St. Nick
Before he was a saint—when he was still just 'Nick'
And he'd be a Turk—dark skin, black mustache, fez

And imagine
Just imagine
What you could tell him
About what the future
Holds in store
For him

(3)

Longest cab ride of my life
But we make it
And I tip really big, just to get out the door that much faster

And never, in all my years of riding BC Ferries, have I seen so many people
    lined up to buy walk-on tickets

Six looooong lines
Pick one

(2)

Golden!
Beautiful, beautiful Golden, BC

Can't stop, though—someone might see the tags on the plates
Press on

Kicking Horse Pass, here I come

(1)

Listen to this Nick, listen to this
In the future, not only will you be canonized, you'll be the most famous
        Catholic saint of them all
But no one will know any real thing about you
No one will know you're from Turkey—that will be novelty information
Everyone will think you're from the North Pole
And that you still live there—thousands of years from now
In a big house
Full of elves
And that all you do all year
Is build toys

(3)

Guaranteed the line you choose is gonna be the slowest one
Every fucking time!!!

But soon I'm right near the ticket window

And a woman
In a reflective orange vest with a walkie-talkie comes out
And says

"The last ferry is full"

(2)

And whoosh!

Green van goes by again
Same green van
Must've stopped in Golden

Good luck again, pal

His tail-lights disappear up ahead, around the corner

(1)

And in their pictures of you—their moving pictures
Which is an art form that hasn't been invented yet
From a country that hasn't been invented yet
In their movies you won't look Turkish at all
You will be a Fat, Jolly, Laughing, Old White guy
Whitest white guy *ever!*
White hair
White beard
White skin
Red nose
Red cheeks
Red hat
Big red suit
With a great big buckle

(3)

"We've sold all the tickets to account for all the life jackets on the ferry
We apologize for the inconvenience, but that's it.
You'll all have to go home now
I'm sorry"

And then a buzz from her walkie-talkie

(2)

Up ahead, around the corner
Two vehicles, spun out into the ditch on the side of the opposite side of
     the road
Crunched in front ends
One of them is not a car
It's a van
It's the Green Van!!

(1)

And every year, once a year
To help celebrate the Birth of Christ
You'll ride through the air
In a sleigh
Drawn by Flying Reindeer

(2)

That just happened
The Green Van just passed me!!
It just crashed!

And right at that exact moment

All nine tabs of Gravol

Kick

In

(3)

"We can take three more people from each line"

I'm third

(1)

And you land on the roof of every house
In the World
And squeeze your big fat roly-poly body through
The *chimney*
With your big fat sack of presents too
And leave a few of them scattered under a tree—a perfectly healthy young
    evergreen tree that the family chopped, dragged in and decorated with
    tinsel and balls
If—and only if—you have checked on your Great Big List
Twice
And judged that the children in that house
To have been Nice that year

(2)

O God
Suddenly I'm seventeen and with my acid-head friends in Burnaby again
Oh Christ

If that Green Van didn't make it
Lord Have Mercy on a little chicken like me . . .

(1)

You will be more integral to the celebration of the birth of Christ
Than Christ Himself!

(3)

I would like One Ticket to Victoria, Please
And the woman says
"Lemme warn ya
It's rough
We almost had to cancel the sailing because of the storm
It still may not be able to dock in Victoria"

I'll risk it

(1)

And they'll call you
An American phonetic mispronunciation
Of the German/Dutch equivalent
Of your canonized Turkish name

(3)

I get on the boat, we leave the dock
Whoa—that woman wasn't whistling Dixie—it's rough
The boat's wobbling from side to side
Like there's a drunken wagoneer at the wheel
I haven't been seasick since I was a kid . . . but . . . but . . .

(2)

Suddenly the pavement just looks wet
Wet?
And the car in front of me fishtails and spins out of control into the snow-
     bank for no reason at all

Black Ice!

(1)

They'll call you
Santa
Claus

(3)

I think I'm . . .

(2)

gonna be . . .

(1)

And what do you think an earnest young Turkish Catholic
would say to all that?

I think I'm gonna be sick . . .

(falls on the floor, vomits

Blackout—snap, the clip lights stay on
Fade music out—10 count)

(2)

And then there's lights

Red lights

Lots of 'em

Moving

This long, slow procession of cars heading east
I catch up to the end
A car catches up behind me
Two more behind him
We all join the parade
Going exactly twenty kilometres an hour
If you speed up, you'll spin out
If you slow down, you'll spin out
If you stay exactly at twenty, you still might spin out

We all know it's black ice
We all know that any of us could be snatched off the road
At any time
For no reason whatsoever

There's no traction
There's no salt
There's no sand
The road has not been ploughed

I have no snow tires
No chains
And no insurance

There's no lights
Except for the headlights of the cars in the rearview mirror
And the red lights from the cars up ahead

And I switch off the radio

And never in my life have I felt so awake

So alive

It goes on like this for hours

We're going the speed of a wagon train
But we're going

It's all about

Patience

Patience

(3)

The water stays rough the whole way

As we near Victoria they make the announcement:
"Folks, we may have to turn back, the storm is too rough. We may not be
    able to dock—we're gonna try, but we may have to turn back to
    Sawassen"

everyone groans

Why does he have to call it "Sawassen"?

Shit
I phoned my girlfriend, I ruined the surprise, she's waiting at the terminal
I can see the terminal

It's right there
Oh please
We are so close
We're So Close

We try to dock once

No go

We try again

Uh-uh
The third time

we . . .

Make it

Everyone cheers
Rushes up to the passenger exit on the promenade deck
We're lined up like fillies at the gate of the Kentucky Derby

Patience

Patience

As the little ramp lowers

And the woman in the reflective orange vest

Draws back

The rope

(1)

I'm okay

I'm okay

I just ate something that didn't agree with me, that's all

I'm gonna go for a walk

But I'll be back

Cuz I'm okay

Sorry about the mess

So I leave the Christmas party and outside
it's snowing
First snow of the year
These big puffy fat flakes that look orange in the streetlight
Like the Christmas episode of a sitcom

But the note
Marty's note
Shit

Ah, let's read it
What the hell
Now's a perfect time

(2)

The first exit comes, a few cars take it
But I don't know where it goes—there's snow caked all over the sign
And it looks just as bad as the highway

Wait 'til Banff
Hang on, boy, wait 'til Banff

Few more hours later
Coming up near Banff

The sky starts turning purple
then pink
then orange

Sunrise in the Rockies

And at the Banff exit

There is sand

Sand?

Hallelujah!

The Road Is Sanded!

And then sanded and ploughed,
And then sanded and ploughed and well-lit

I stay on the highway
A few cars try and join us on the on-ramp from Banff
Cocky drivers, going full speed
You sons-a bitches, who do you think you are?
We stay at twenty

Not in front-a me you don't!

Then we all speed up
But just a bit

Then a bit more

Then there's two lanes
We start to pass each other

And as you pass you can see the faces of the other drivers
And you can instantly tell which are the Johnny-Come-Latelys from Banff
        and which are the whole-timers
Because the whole-timers have all got the badge
The mark from that night-long procession over the black ice
You can see it in the face

And the best part is
None of us will ever meet

(3)

I speed into the terminal right at the front of the pack

and and and

there she was

There She Was

(switches off the green clip light)

(2)

By the time we get to Calgary there's no snow at all—on the road, side of
the road, falling from the sky, anywhere

People are walking around like it's just a normal day
And I guess it is
It's even kinda nice out

It's nine AM
I haven't slept a wink
and I don't care

I find the address on the insurance form
Park
Walk up the steps
Ring the bell

A woman answers

Are you Sheila Sanderson?

"Yes"

Good

Do you recognize that van parked in front of your house?

"Yes"

I just drove it here from Vancouver
It's a long story
Could you sign this, where the X is?

She does

Thanks

Bye

"Bye"

I own it!
I take it to an insurance agency and insure it for one day

I make the rounds of the Calgary used-car dealers

They don't want it

It's a good van, one of 'em tells me, but there's just no market for 'em

I know. I know.

Everyone drives SUVs these days
"Tell you what though. You could take it to a scrap dealer, they'd strip it for
     parts, maybe give ya fifty bucks or somethin'
The windshield's still pretty good"

(*pause*)

And then I get
Maybe the best idea
I've ever had

I drive to the library
And ask at the desk
If they have phone books for other cities

(1)

"Why don't you stay with us?
You can rent the guest room for December and January for

$200 a month

We don't mind
It's no problem at all
We'd love to have you

And we don't mean that
As a euphemism

Signed
Marty & Tina"

(switches off the blue clip light)

(2)

I pull into Lethbridge
Two hours south of Calgary
Two hours . . .
I've been driving all night
I'm waaaaay past being tired
Two hours is like five minutes

It's mid-afternoon, the sun is out and bright and warm
It's melted the black ice
now it really is just what it looked like the whole time:
Wet pavement

And this goddam van
I've been driving it since yesterday afternoon
Through snow and black ice
Through city driving in Vancouver and Calgary
Through the Coast Mountains, the Kootenay Mountains, the Rocky
    Mountains
And all stops in between
And it's purring like a calico kitten
Good ol' van
Failed inspection, my ass

I find the address I wrote down at the library
It's not hard
Lethbridge isn't that big

I walk up to the steps
Ring the bell

Please be home

Door opens

Perfect
Exactly like I pictured her

Hello, Margaret

And I throw her the keys

(switches off the red clip light

Curtain call lighting
Sound: bring in "Yes, Jesus Loves Me" at level)

THE END
◞

About the Author

TJ Dawe is a Vancouver-based writer and performer who has toured extensively throughout North America and Australia. In 1998, his play *Tired Clichés* received a Jessie Richardson Award for Best New Play or Musical. In 2001, *The Slip-Knot* received the Just For Laughs Comedy Award in Montreal, was remounted at the Just For Laughs On the Edge series, and won the Best Male Performer award at the 2002 Orlando International Fringe Festival and at the 2001 Victoria Fringe Festival.

His shows, which combine elements of stand-up comedy, music, and physical theatre to explore serious subjects, have drawn comparisons to Lord Buckley, Jerry Seinfeld and Eric Bogosian.

Plays by TJ Dawe

Whank, 1997
Stating the Obvious, 1997
Tired Clichés, 1998
Labrador, 1999
Constable Sparky and the Mystery Pirate Orphan, or *Fort Steele in Flames: a Rolicking Comedy, with Songs*, co-written with Michael Rinaldi, 2000
52 Pick-up, co-written with Rita Bozi, 2000
The Slip-Knot, 2001
The Doctor is Sick, adapted from Anthony Burgess, 2002
Constable Sparky and the Curse of the Hoodwinked Swede, co-written with Michael Rinaldi, 2002
Tracks, adapted from Jack London, 2002
Toothpaste & Cigars, co-written with Michael Rinaldi, 2003
The Power of Ignorance, co-written with Chris Gibbs, 2003
A Canadian Bartender at Butlin's, 2003

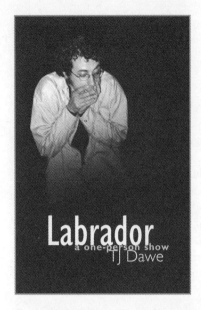

Labrador
a one-person show
TJ Dawe

Labrador is about a part of the world that practically no one knows anything about— Canada's own Siberia. And because your tour guide is the lovely and talented TJ Dawe, it's also about the cycle of generations, how the hell bread got invented, the blurry line between fact and fiction, why "schedule" needs to be pronounced with a "k" sound, and how aliens and archaeologists are the same. And someone in the audience will receive a free banana.

Labrador is not about a dog.
—*Orlando Sentinel* (Florida)

Dawe has storytelling down to a fine art . . . this man's timing and delivery, and the accuracy of his eye on Canada's extremities, are masterful.
—*Vancouver Sun*

All Dawe's considerable talents . . . are on display in this quirky new one-man show about his adventures, both real and imagined, as part of a touring children's show in a part of Canada about which very few of us know anything beyond where it hangs on the map. Funny, endearing stuff.
—*Toronto Sun*